SPOTLIGHT ON
THE
AGE OF
ENLIGHTENMENT

Alan Blackwood

SPOTLIGHT ON HISTORY

Editor: Kerstin Walker
Cover illustration: La Gamme d'Amour by Jean-Antoine Watteau

First published in 1987 by Wayland (Publishers) Ltd
61 Western Road, Hove, East Sussex BN3 1JD, England

British Library Cataloguing in Publication Data
Blackwood, Alan
Spotlight on the age of enlightenment.—(Spotlight on history)
1. Europe—Intellectual life—18th century—Juvenile literature
I. Title   940.2'53   CB411

ISBN 1-85210-009-5

Printed in Great Britain at The Bath Press, Avon

CONTENTS

1 THE SPIRIT OF ENLIGHTENMENT

'**D**are to know!' said the German philosopher Immanuel Kant. 'Dare to use your own intelligence! That is the motto of the Enlightenment!' There have been many people and periods in history that we could call 'enlightened', from the days of ancient China and Confucius to the great flowering of art and literature of the European Renaissance in the fifteenth and sixteenth centuries. Kant's Enlightenment, and the one that is the subject of this book, was that of Europe in the eighteenth century.

To understand better what Kant meant by Enlightenment, we need to look back very briefly into European history. For centuries the Roman Catholic Church had been a dominant force that did not allow any questioning of the doctrines that it propounded. These restrictions encouraged a fatalistic attitude among people, because they were taught that by accepting their hardships and sufferings here on earth,

Galileo's pursuit of truth through scientific discovery led him into conflict with the Roman Catholic Church. His discoveries were an early inspiration to the Age of the Enlightenment.

The first reflecting telescope invented by Sir Isaac Newton, and built with his own hands. His discoveries concerning the universe helped the spread of enlightened ideas.

they could expect a better afterlife. From the start of the Renaissance (about 1400), Church authority was gradually being undermined by people such as Copernicus and Galileo, who put forward new ideas about the universe, René Descartes, who argued that everything should be doubted until it could be proved, and Sir Isaac Newton, who heralded the modern age of science with his laws on gravity and planetary motion. Magnificent new buildings, such as Louis XIV's huge Palace at Versailles, and Sir Christopher Wren's St Paul's Cathedral in London, also stood for an increasingly bold and confident view of this world, and of people's ability to master it.

By the start of the eighteenth century confidence and optimism prevailed among scholars, scientists, writers and artists. Instead of the age-old faith in religion, there was a desire for knowledge, a willingness to exchange new ideas, a belief that rational thought and action could solve every problem. The Enlightenment of eighteenth-century Europe was a period in which a spirit of toleration and reasonableness emerged.

By the close of the century two major events, the French Revolution and the American War of Independence, were seen by many people as encapsulating the essence of the Enlightenment; namely that people were beginning to have a degree of control over their lives.

Diderot's Encyclopédie and Johnson's Dictionary

A work that perfectly summed up the spirit of the age was the *Encyclopédie* of the French scholar and novelist Denis Diderot. With a large team of other scholars to help him, Diderot spent many years compiling his *Encyclopédie*, which was intended to include all existing knowledge of science and astronomy, history, art and architecture, literature, philosophy and music. His motive for compiling this work was, as he put it, 'a love of truth, a passion to do good to others.' By doing good to others, he meant offering them the knowledge by which they could improve themselves, grow in wisdom, and help to make the world a better, happier place for everyone.

Immanuel Kant, the eighteenth-century German philosopher, was one of the important rationalist thinkers of the age.

Dr Samuel Johnson, a leading literary figure of the Enlightenment, is best known for his Dictionary of the English Language.

While Diderot and his team were producing their *Encyclopédie* in Paris, Dr Samuel Johnson was hard at work in London on his *Dictionary of the English Language*. Dr Johnson is much admired as a shining example of an enlightened eighteenth-century man. We know a lot about him as a person, thanks to his almost equally famous biographer, James Boswell. Johnson was, we might now think, a rather eccentric person, with some odd prejudices and ideas; but essentially he was a kind, tolerant, and witty man, and one who could see through the hypocrisy and foolishness of others. 'Patriotism', he said on one occasion, 'is the last refuge of the scoundrel.' What he was implying was that scoundrels will often try to get round people by appealing to their emotions and clouding their judgments. His Dictionary is full of such shrewd epigrams, in which a few well-chosen words say a great deal. It, too, is a testament to the Enlightenment.

The spread of enlightened ideas was something that affected only the wealthy, and had very little relevance for the poor and sick.

In the countryside labourers and peasants were often dependent on the goodwill and generosity of the landowners to help relieve their poverty-stricken living conditions.

A good life for the few

It is important for us to keep things in perspective. Europe in the eighteenth century did not, in reality, suddenly become a kind of utopia, a place where everybody was happy and free, and life was easy. For the majority of its people, life remained hard. Many were tied to the land, labouring for the landowning classes, often with barely enough food and clothing for themselves; or they were crowded together in towns and cities, where there was no proper sanitation, and where poverty, vice and squalor were rife. During the course of the century, in a few countries, the first steps were taken in the direction of public health, primary education for all and penal reform. But by the end of the eighteenth century, most people were still illiterate and many died young, like the majority of people in earlier times, from malnutrition and disease. Despite the emergence of humanity and toleration that were supposed to be the hallmark of the age, people could still be left to rot in foul prisons for the slightest offence, be clamped in the stocks or pillory, or publicly hanged to the shouts and jeers of the mob.

A man in the pillory at Charing Cross, London. Such punishments were commonplace and attracted large crowds, who enjoyed these public humiliations.

The Age of Enlightenment, as we have described it, was the province mainly of the aristocracy, wealthy landowners, merchants and bankers. It was they alone who had the time and money to indulge their interests in history, science, philosophy, fine art, literature and music. Such people paid scholars, artists and musicians to instruct and entertain them. Patronage of the arts and of learning flourished in the eighteenth century as never before or since. 'Philosophy has no apostles more well disposed than the grand seigneurs', said one lady of the time, referring to the French upper classes.

What may seem surprising is that even scholarly and liberal-minded men like Diderot and Johnson were, on the whole, prepared to participate in this system. They, together with all other educated people of the age, talked much about living in a better and more beautiful world. However, it should be emphasized that they were not social reformers. They and their wealthy and often royal patrons were, for the most part, content to defend and maintain their privileges in life. The Age of Enlightenment was, therefore, of real relevance only to the educated and upper classes of European society.

The Royal Academy Exhibition in London. Patronage of the arts and of learning was the preserve of the rich, for whom such events were both cultural and social.

2 THE PHILOSOPHERS

Of all those who helped to create the spirit of eighteenth-century Enlightenment, it was the scholars and philosophers who led the field. They did not transform the world overnight, but much of what they thought and wrote did have a deep and lasting effect, not only upon the social and political climate of their own times, but upon the course of events right up to the present day.

The French 'philosophes'
The largest single group of scholars and thinkers were the French philosophers—the *philosophes*. It was a rather loose word to apply to them. They did not form one special 'school' of philosophy—one group of thinkers devoted to the same ideas. Indeed, some of them were not really philosophers at all. But they nearly all shared the belief, held so firmly by the earlier French philosopher Descartes, that truth was man's highest ideal, and that it could be arrived at by thinking and acting objectively and rationally.

The leading figure among the *philosophes* was François-Marie Arouet, whose pen name was Voltaire. 'I disagree with everything you say, but will defend to the death your right to say it!' is the most famous quotation attributed to him. He spent much time, as did the other *philosophes*, attacking the Church. According to Voltaire the Church stood in the way of truth by telling people what to believe instead of allowing them to think for themselves. He also criticized it for being a powerful institution, which often acted hypocritically in order to defend the many vested interests which it held. Voltaire was a waspish little man who used satire and wit to sting his opponents. He wrote thousands of letters, pamphlets and essays, often defending people whom he believed were the victims of bigotry or injustice. Many of his plays and novels, such as *Candide*, ridiculed life's follies, and, at a more scholarly level, he contributed to Diderot's *Encyclopédie*, and wrote a history of civilization.

The Baron Charles de Montesquieu was closer to being a true philosopher. He concentrated on political ideas. 'Republics come to an end through luxury, monarchies through poverty', he said, referring back to the decline of the ancient republics of Greece and Rome, and, with great foresight, forward to the collapse of the bankrupt French monarchy before the end of the century. With his knowledge of history and his own experience as a lawyer, Montesquieu argued that there

MARIE FRANÇOIS AROUET DE VOLTAIRE

POST GENTIIS HIC CARUS ERIT,
NUNC CARUS AMICIS.

Voltaire was a leading philosophe *who believed that the pursuit of truth and rational thought were the highest ideals for mankind.*

Voltaire's famous short story Candide *is a satirical masterpiece ridiculing human weaknesses. This illustration shows one of the central characters in it, Doctor Pangloss.*

was no single, perfect form of government, but that due examination of the facts—historical, social, economic—would point to the best form of government for each nation. 'Useless laws weaken necessary laws', was another of his observations, as true today as it was then.

Jeremy Bentham, the British philosopher, believed that people were rational beings and that they would act in the best interests of society.

'Man is born free, but everywhere he is in chains', declared Jean-Jacques Rousseau at the start of his great political testament *Le Contrat Social*. Rousseau believed that men and women were by nature good ('The Noble Savage' was another of his phrases), but that they were corrupted by society. Given that people needed to live in societies, it was up to them to enter into a 'social contract', by which they surrendered their natural freedoms but gained a new, collective freedom in return. The way in which Rousseau wrestled with his own ideas, and the radical changes he proposed, foreshadowed the French Revolution and the industrial and political unrest of the nineteenth century. Some students of politics also contend that Rousseau's ideas about the sacrifice of individual freedom to the higher collective will of the state foreshadow the totalitarian regimes of Stalin, Hitler and other dictators of the twentieth century, though Rousseau himself undoubtedly would have been horrified by such developments.

Utilitarianism
British government, as we can read in more detail on page 53, was widely admired for the manner in which it had managed to strike a balance between king and parliament by the time of the eighteenth century. Though the system was not perfect, there were not the same glaring weaknesses of government as there were, for example, in the

Jean-Jacques Rousseau, the French philosopher, whose writings helped inspire the ideas behind the French Revolution.

France of Louis XV. The growth of empire and development of trade were far more important issues for the philosophers to discuss, inspiring some important new thinking.

The Britons Adam Smith and Jeremy Bentham agreed with another of the French *philosophes*, Claude Helvétius, that people act only out of self-interest. They applied this principle to the utilitarian subject of trade and economics. In his book *An Inquiry into the Nature and Causes of the Wealth of Nations*, Smith presented the case for a system of trade and economics known by the French term 'laissez-faire'. According to Smith every man should do what was in his best interest, in terms of work and trade, and as a result productivity and wealth would soon increase. Free trade between nations would stimulate wealth still further. All this may seem reasonable enough today, but it was radical thinking in the eighteenth century, when most wealth (capital) was still jealously guarded by a few kings and rich landowners. Bentham, for his part, pointed out that the self-interest of individuals and of whole nations were not necessarily the same. The essential principle of Bentham's philosophy was that man should be guided by the need to produce the greatest good for the greatest number. This, he believed, would bring about a fair distribution of wealth.

Although they were more interested in money and trade than in political justice and freedom, Smith and Bentham believed just as strongly as other thinkers of the Age of Enlightenment that man was a rational being, and that through clear thought and reasonable action the quality of life for mankind could be improved.

16

Empiricism

In addition to the French *philosophes* and the British utilitarians, there were the empiricists, who argued that everything should be doubted that could not be checked against the evidence of our physical senses. A word, said the Scottish philosopher David Hume, has no real meaning if it cannot be related to something we have personally experienced. Another empirical philosopher, the Irishman George Berkeley, even doubted the existence of an object such as a tree or a house, if we could not see or touch it for ourselves.

Such were the extraordinarily varied, sometimes conflicting patterns of eighteenth-century thought, which Immanuel Kant wished to relate to the whole body of human knowledge and experience. Perhaps the fact that he spent almost the whole of his life in the East Prussian city of Königsberg (now Kaliningrad in the USSR), far removed from the great intellectual centres like London and Paris, helped him to see everything in a clearer perspective. In a series of celebrated 'Critiques', Kant explored all aspects of philosophy, reason, morality, empiricism and aesthetics (the analysis of art and beauty). He accepted that many of his writings might be difficult to grasp, but pointed out that seeking the truth was never a simple task. Kant also put forward a theory about the origins of the solar system, and he proposed a political federation of states to prevent war. After the First World War, the League of Nations tried to put such an idea into practice. And again, after the Second World War, the same idea was tried by the United Nations. Although such an ideal has yet to be achieved, it says much for the enlightened outlook of eighteenth-century thinkers that Kant should at least have thought it possible.

The Woolwich dockyards near London were an important trading centre. Utilitarians argued that free trade would bring about a fair distribution of wealth, and that this was in the best interests of everyone.

3 THE WRITER'S CRAFT

One of the greatest books of the eighteenth century was *Decline and Fall of the Roman Empire* by the English scholar Edward Gibbon. His beautifully written Roman history marked a tremendous revival of interest in the civilizations of the ancient world among people of the Enlightenment. British writers of the period also did a great deal to establish the new literary form of the novel, which, by and large, was a more substantial piece of work than most novels written today.

The novel
The novel—the word means something new, fresh, original—flourished in eighteenth-century Britain, largely as a result of a growing middle-class that had the leisure and the money to buy books. Also, there was no radio or television to compete with books in the home.

Many novels, with their witty and satirical comments on society, covered much the same ground as the work of the philosophers. They were 'didactic' works, meant to instruct as well as to entertain. One of the most famous is *Gulliver's Travels* by Jonathan Swift, an Englishman born and brought up in Ireland. Most people now think of it as a children's story. Swift, however, intended it as a hard-hitting satire on human folly. Gulliver's first journey, to Lilliput, shows how absurd human behaviour can seem when acted out by a society of midgets. His next visit, to Brobdignag, views the human race through the eyes of giants. 'The most pernicious race of little odious vermin that nature ever suffered to crawl upon the surface of the earth!' is the verdict of the king of Brobdignag.

One remarkable novel of the time was Lawrence Sterne's *The Life and Opinions of Tristram Shandy*, an entertaining comedy, which also contained many philosophical reflections. 'The desire of knowledge, like the thirst of riches, increases ever with the acquisition of it', is one of them. Sterne, incidentally, was allowed to travel to the South of France for his health, even when Britain and France were at war, which is an indication of how highly writers and scholars were esteemed everywhere in eighteenth-century Europe.

Other novels came closer to the modern idea of the novel as a straightforward work of fiction. Daniel Defoe, whose own life as a

Jonathan Swift's famous novel Gulliver's Travels *is one of the greatest satirical writings in the English language.*

Gulliver captured by the Lilliputians in Gulliver's Travels. *Swift used the tiny Lilliputians to represent the small-mindedness of people.*

soldier, government agent and political pamphleteer was colourful enough for any story, wrote two famous adventure novels. *Robinson Crusoe* was inspired by the shipwreck and rescue from a desert island of a real sailor named Alexander Selkirk. In fact, most people now know this book only in an abridged form and so miss the social and philosophical comment of the original version. *Moll Flanders* is the story of a girl, told in her own words, who is born in prison and forced into a life of crime in London before transportation to the American colony of Virginia. Henry Fielding's *The Adventures of Tom Jones* and Oliver Goldsmith's *The Vicar of Wakefield* also cast light on different aspects of eighteenth-century English life.

The frontispiece to the First Edition of Robinson Crusoe, *a convincing and vivid account of the adventures of a shipwrecked man.*

Another important English novelist was Samuel Richardson. His novels were often made up entirely of letters exchanged between the principal characters. Some were translated into French by the Abbé Prevost, whose own *Manon Lescaut*, a romantic tale of love leading to tragedy, later inspired several operas.

Poetry and plays

The poet Alexander Pope said, 'the proper study of mankind is man.' He turned his attention to the fashionable society of his own time and place. The people who belonged to it were living in a more liberal, permissive society than any before them. In some respects they behaved more reasonably towards each other, and yet, in others their social

Daniel Defoe led an exciting and varied life, which enabled him to write some highly popular adventure stories. He only started his new career as a fiction writer at the age of 60.

A scene from Tom Jones, *a sometimes riotous account of English eighteenth-century life. This illustration shows Tom Jones rescuing the heroine Sophia.*

freedom encouraged them to behave with extra frivolity. Pope mocked them in extremely polished and amusing poems, such as *The Rape of the Lock* and *Verses to the Memory of an Unfortunate Lady*. The other major British poet of the age was the Scotsman Robert Burns. He, too, could write satirical verse in the best English tradition of the period, such as *The Cotters's Saturday Night* and *Death and Dr Hornbrook*. He also helped to revive Scottish pride after the Jacobite

23

THE WAY OF THE WORLD.

A COMEDY. IN FIVE ACTS.—BY WILLIAM CONGREVE.

Lady W.—"Oh, heavens! what's this?—Act iv, scene 1.

Persons Represented.

Sir Wilful Witwould.	Witwould.	Lady Wishfort.	Mrs. Fainall.
Fainall.	Petulant.	Mrs. Millamant	Foible.
Mirabell.	Waitwell.	Mrs. Marwood.	Mincing.

ACT I.

SCENE I.—A Chocolate House.

MIRABLE and FAINALL, rising from cards; BETTY waiting.

Mir. You are a fortunate man, Mr. Fainall.

Fain. Have we done?

Mir. What you please. I'll play on, to entertain you.

Fain. No, I'll give you your revenge another time, when you are not so indifferent; you are thinking of something else now, and play too negligently; the coldness of a losing gamester lessens the pleasure of the winner. I'd no more play with a man that slighted his ill fortune, than I'd make love to a woman who undervalued the loss of her reputation.

Mir. You have a case extremely delicate, and are for refining on your pleasures.

Fain. Pr'ythee, why so reserved? Something has put thee out of humour.

Mir. Not at all. I happen to be grave to-day; and you are gay, that's all.

Fain. Confess, Millamant and you quarrelled last night, after I left you; my fair cousin has some humours that would tempt the patience of a stoic. What, some coxcomb came in, and was well received by her, while you were by?

Mir. Witwould and Petulant! And what was worse, her aunt, your wife's mother, my evil

No. 102.—Dicks' British Drama.

The Way of the World by William Congreve was a satirical play, which mocked the manners and weaknesses of fashionable society.

THE SCHOOL FOR SCANDAL.

A COMEDY, IN FIVE ACTS.—BY R. B. SHERIDAN.

Sir Peter.—"LADY TEAZLE, BY ALL THAT'S DAMNABLE."—*Act* iv, *scene* 3.

Sheridan's play The School for Scandal *was extremely popular because of the clever and pleasing way it mocked English society and encouraged audiences to laugh at themselves.*

defeats of 1715 and 1745 at the hands of the English army, with many beautiful poems, such as *Auld Lang Syne*, written in Lowland Scots dialect.

Many eighteenth-century plays were comparable to Pope's verse in the way they portrayed and mocked the manners and foibles of fashionable society. They are known as 'comedies of manners'. In 1700 appeared *The Way of the World* by William Congreve, its title suggesting a tolerant, worldly-wise attitude to human affairs. Goldsmith, who wrote one successful novel, also wrote one successful play with *She Stoops to Conquer*, another classic comedy of manners.

The master of this kind of play was Richard Brinsley Sheridan, who was an Anglo-Irishman, as was Swift. Sheridan was one of the most colourful figures of eighteenth-century London; he was a manager of the famous Drury Lane Theatre, and was also actively involved in politics. As a playwright, he knew exactly how to amuse his audiences, by caricaturing them upon the stage. In line with theatrical custom, Sheridan gave the characters in his plays names that exactly fitted their type. The characters Joseph Surface and Lady Teazle appear in *The School for Scandal*, and in *The Rivals* there is Lydia Languish and Mrs Malaprop, the scatterbrained lady who is always mixing up her words. 'Illiterate him, I say, quite from your memory', is one of her famous lines, as is, 'He is the very pineapple of politeness!' The word 'malapropism' for such hilarious blunders is now a part of the English language.

There were the equivalents of the English comedy of manners in other countries. In France, where there was state censorship, Pierre Beaumarchais went to prison for satirizing the aristocracy in *The Barber of Seville* and *The Marriage of Figaro* (both destined to become even more famous as operas by Rossini and Mozart, respectively). In Italy, Carlo Goldoni based his comedies on the far older traditions of the comedia dell'arte, with its characters such as Harlequin and Pulcinella acting out their parts to ritual displays of emotion.

Journalism

By the eighteenth century, London was a city with a population of over one million people, but it was still compact enough for politicians, artists, musicians, writers and other notable figures in society to meet each other regularly at dinner parties, at the theatre, and in the coffee houses that were then at the height of fashion. In 1764 the Literary Club was set up in London and attracted many talented writers. In fact one of its founder members was Dr Johnson. Gossip and intrigue at such meeting-places helped the growth of journalism.

Magazines and the earliest kinds of newspaper carried literary criticism and social and political comment. Two important journals were *The Gentleman's Magazine*, which was edited by Dr Johnson, and the *Spectator*, which was founded by two masters of the literary form of the essay, Richard Steele and Joseph Addison. The *Spectator* is still published today. Swift and Defoe, at the centre of London politics and social life, also wrote for these magazines. Another journal of the time, *The North Briton*, made history when it carried a defamatory article against George III written by a politician named John Wilkes. This resulted in a constitutional crisis that confirmed the shift of power from monarch to parliament, which is a subject that is discussed again in more detail on page 53.

In Paris, Voltaire, Diderot and the other *philosophes* were equally industrious writers of pamphlets and journals. The two cities of Paris and London were the European centres of literature in the eighteenth-century and for a long time to come.

Coffee houses were used by fashionable people as meeting-places for political discussion and the exchange of literary and artistic ideas.

4 ARCHITECTS AND ARTISTS

During the long period of the Middle Ages, the great civilizations of ancient or Classical Greece and Rome were largely forgotten. From the time of the Renaissance, people took a fresh interest in them, and especially in the ruins of their beautiful temples and other monuments. The columns and pediments of such edifices inspired a new kind of European architecture. Some of the new buildings, such as St Peter's Basilica in Rome, were built on the grandest scale, known as the Baroque style. By the eighteenth century, the grandeur of Baroque architecture was giving way to styles of building, either more fanciful or more restrained and elegant, in keeping with the relaxed and cultivated spirit of the age.

Place de la Concorde in Paris is a fine example of the spaciousness and order of eighteenth-century town planning.

Blenheim Palace, built for the Duke of Marlborough by Sir John Vanbrugh, is set in magnificent landscaped gardens.

Rococo and classical buildings

Rococo building and design expressed the sense of sheer pleasure in living that came with the eighteenth century. Inside, such buildings were richly decorated with marble, and with plaster work moulded into elaborate twists and curls and painted light blues, pinks and golds, giving the impression of soft, sunlit clouds. The Rococo style began in France and Italy, but was enthusiastically taken up by such people as Frederick the Great of Prussia in his summer palace of *Sans Souci* ('Carefree') at Potsdam, and reached its peak in many of the palaces and churches of Switzerland, Austria and Bavaria.

The main architectural style of the eighteenth century, however, was called Neo (New)-Classical, or Classical Revival. The columns and pediments of Classical antiquity, mentioned above, created a kind of geometry in buildings that was suited to an age that prided itself on its sense of order and reason. The stage was set for this style well before the eighteenth century, by a building called 'The Rotunda', near Vicenza, in Italy. The architect was Andrea Palladio, and the numerous buildings modelled on it are called 'Palladian', as well as being Neo-Classical.

An outstanding example of the Neo-Classical style in England is Blenheim Palace, designed by Sir John Vanbrugh for the Duke of Marlborough. It stands in parkland laid out by Lancelot 'Capability' Brown, a landscape artist who aimed, in the same Classical spirit, to create a perfect harmony between the works of man and of nature. In what was then colonial America, Thomas Jefferson, principal author of the Declaration of Independence and a future president (see page 64), designed several buildings in the same Classical or Palladian style, including his own home in Virginia.

In towns and cities, architects liked to design buildings as part of some larger plan, that was both spacious and well ordered. The Place de la Concorde in Paris, the Royal Crescent in Bath, the centres of Edinburgh and Dublin, and many of London's streets and squares, are fine examples of eighteenth-century architecture and town planning. In Britain it is often referred to as Georgian architecture, after the names of the reigning monarchs of the time.

Interior decoration

No expense was spared to make such buildings as splendid inside as they were outside. Some of the finest interiors in Britain in the eighteenth century were those designed by the Scottish architect Robert Adam. Special features of his work included slender, curving staircases, domed skylights, ceilings, floors and fireplaces. He used soft, pastel shades of blue, pink or green, like Rococo artists, but applied them to Grecian pillars and other Classical motifs, creating a mood of cool, lofty elegance. In Russia, Catherine the Great's summer palace at *Tsarskoe Selo* (now Pushkino), near Leningrad, was decorated in the same spirit of Classical elegance and restraint.

Tsarskoe Selo, the summer palace of Catherine the Great of Russia, was built in the new Rococo style of architecture, showing how far across Europe the ideas of the Enlightenment had spread.

The centre of Edinburgh, the capital of Scotland, is well-ordered, light and spacious. This picture shows Waterloo Place, Nelson's Monuments and Carlton Hill.

Just as much care was lavished on individual items. Large mirrors in gilded frames reflected the glittering light from chandeliers. Clocks, notably French ones, were made as delicately as jewellery. In England, Thomas Chippendale, Thomas Sheraton and George Hepplewhite made it a golden age for furniture design, with tables, chairs and other items both more functional and more elegantly constructed than any furniture before or since the eighteenth century. The American William Savery was a master craftsman influenced by the new trends in Europe. The finest pottery and porcelain, including dinner and tea-sets, and ornamental figurines from the factories of Sèvres in France, Meissen in Germany, and Josiah Wedgwood in England were produced at this time. A new interest in Chinese and Japanese art, inspired by the growing trade with the Far East, produced a style in some European pottery and porcelain called chinoiserie.

The Royal Crescent in Bath, the supreme example of Georgian architecture, gives a sense of elegance and harmony. It complements many other Georgian buildings in the city.

The painters

The Italian artist Giovanni Tiepolo established the closest possible connection between architecture and art by decorating the interiors of Rococo churches and palaces with frescoes (wall paintings) as gorgeous as the buildings themselves. In France, Jean-Antoine Watteau and François Boucher, together with other Rococo artists painted pictures of soft, idyllic landscapes, and designed settings for *Fêtes galantes*, which were the summer evening entertainments laid on for Louis XV's court in the lovely gardens of Versailles.

However, many of the best-known artists of the period were portrait painters. It was considered a mark of prestige for the upper classes and aristocracy to have their portraits painted, indicating the extent of their wealth and power. Francisco Goya was official portrait painter to the Spanish court, although his greatest work was in a very different style, belonging to that of the early nineteenth century. Jean-Honoré Fragonard delighted the French court with his light-hearted and graceful portrayals of aristocratic life. John Singleton Copley painted more sober portraits of people in colonial America.

In England, the most successful artists of the period were all portrait painters, the most important being Sir Joshua Reynolds, Thomas Gainsborough and George Romney. A feature of their portraits, when compared with those of earlier times, is how the aristocratic clients of these English artists liked to be pictured in a relaxed and informal pose, often leaning against a gate or mantelpiece. Gainsborough also liked to set his portraits in a landscape, clearly showing that by the eighteenth century much of rural England had been transformed into a gentle pattern of woods, fields and hedgerows.

The other major English artist of the period, William Hogarth, gave a very different impression of eighteenth-century life. He was closer in style to Swift and Defoe, than to Reynolds and Gainsborough, in pointing out, as no artist had done before him, human weakness and ignorance. Hogarth concentrated on illustrating the vices and miseries

Function and elegance are combined in these chairs, designed by the English craftsman Thomas Sheraton.

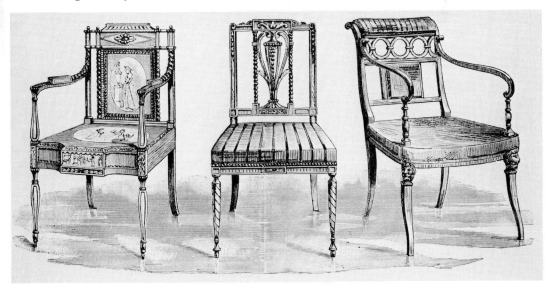

of the age, such as the ruination of poor people by the sale of cheap gin, which the wealthy and privileged members of society tried to ignore. In addition to paintings he also produced many engravings, which were sold in black and white reproductions to those who could not afford a painting. It was the success of these engravings which helped to make Hogarth a pioneer of popular art.

The French Rococo artist Watteau often painted landscapes, which captured the fanciful and idyllic spirit of the French aristocracy at leisure.

A study for a portrait by Gainsborough. The English portrait painters were some of the most accomplished of the age.

Gin Lane, *one of the many graphic engravings by William Hogarth,*
warning against the dangers of excessive drinking of gin.

5 MUSIC

Music flourished in the eighteenth century. It was considered the most civilizing of all the arts, by those of wealth and good taste. It was also the biggest status symbol of the age. Certainly it was a mark of status to possess a library or to have your portrait painted, but only the most privileged had both the money and the premises to maintain an orchestra, to play at meal times and serenade guests. Such a state of affairs brought with it new musical forms, styles and methods of performance that represented some of the biggest changes in the whole art of music for nearly a thousand years. And while many of the outstanding philosophers and writers, architects and painters of the time were French, British or Italian, it was the German-speaking countries that showed the way forward in music.

From voices to instruments
At the beginning of the eighteenth century, the two greatest composers were Johann Sebastian Bach and George Frederick Handel. Bach stayed in his native land of Germany, spending his whole career in aristocratic or church employment. He wrote music in nearly every existing form and style, but is remembered above all for his great choral works, including the *St John* and *St Matthew* Passions, which follow a tradition of church choral music going back as far as the Middle Ages. Handel was also German by birth, but spent most of his life in London, composing operas in the opulent Baroque style that had started about a hundred years earlier in Italy. When this went out of fashion with London audiences, he composed *Messiah* and other oratorios, which were still similar to his operas but were based on Bible stories and so were thought more respectable.

Changes in music, however, were already on the way. Bach's grand but rather austere choral style gave way to singing of a lighter, brighter character. Handel's spectacular Baroque-style operas were followed by those of Christoph Willibald Gluck, much more serious and dignified in tone, and those of Wolfgang Amadeus Mozart, which brought to opera real-life comedy and drama. But most notable was the growing interest in purely instrumental music. This was largely inspired by the desire of kings, queens and princes all to have their own private band of musicians.

The German states became the centre of all this new musical activity, because the country was still divided up politically into dozens of

A musical afternoon in a Paris salon was as much a social event as for serious music-making.

kingdoms and principalities, each boasting its own court orchestra, and possibly also an opera house. Frederick the Great brought to his Potsdam court a very talented group of musicians, including Carl Philipp Emanuel Bach, one of the sons of J. S. Bach. There was another very fine court orchestra in the Rhineland town of Mannheim. Dr Charles Burney, an English scholar who made a musical tour of Europe, called it 'An Army of Generals!', because, in his opinion, each member of the orchestra was a top-class player.

The new classical music
The eighteenth century was a fascinating musical age not simply because of the change of emphasis from vocal and choral to instrumental and orchestral music. The new kinds of music that developed were important in marking a break with the past. Antonio Vivaldi and other Italian composers showed the potential that existed for brilliant playing with the newly-invented violin 'family' of instruments. They also created a new kind of orchestral piece called a 'concerto'. Two other noteworthy composers, the Frenchman François Couperin and the

Italian Domenico Scarlatti, were both masters of the harpsichord, and steered music away from the long-established polyphonic style—the building up of a piece from a single theme or melody—and towards a much more structured and clearer type of music.

George Frederick Handel, the greatest composer of Baroque opera and oratorio, who spent most of his life in London.

A less reverent view of the new English passion for oratorios as depicted by Hogarth.

The most significant result of these trends in music was the emergence of the sonata form. This was a way of writing music with several themes, and several clearly defined sections, all linked neatly together to form one continuous piece. It was a very well constructed musical form, allowing composers to fit more ideas into a single piece of music than had ever before been possible. As well as the sonata form itself, composers began writing larger works made up of several individual pieces, or 'movements', nicely contrasted with each other in terms of rhythm, speed and mood. Such compositions, for one or two instruments, were called sonatas. For an orchestra they were called symphonies, a word taken from a type of overture to an opera or play, called a 'sinfonia'.

Mozart performing before the Austrian Emperor, Joseph II. Nearly all musicians of the time needed a wealthy patron to make a living.

Joseph Haydn, who worked at the Austrian court, did more than anybody else to create the new Classical form of the symphony and the string quartet.

In their carefully constructed manner of composition, and the well-balanced sound they called for, these new forms were the musical equivalent of the handsomely-proportioned Neo-Classical buildings of the eighteenth century. Thus, sonata form, sonatas and symphonies mark the age of Classical music—the true music of the Enlightenment.

Haydn and Mozart

From the middle of the eighteenth century, many composers turned to writing the new Classical music, experimenting constantly with even better methods of musical construction and a clear balance of sound. The master of them all was Joseph Haydn. He spent much of his career as musical director at a princely court, not in Germany itself, but in the neighbouring Hapsburg (or Austrian) Empire. His prime duty was to write operas and church and dance music for court occasions, but he too had a good orchestra at his disposal, and over the years he composed many symphonies and string quartets (like miniature symphonies for the perfect balance of two violins, viola and cello). At the height of his fame Haydn made two visits to London, for which he composed two new sets of symphonies which were to be the last and finest of his career. Most have nicknames. There is, for example, the 'Surprise' Symphony, so named because of an unexpected loud chord in the quiet slow movement. Haydn had a lively sense of humour. 'That'll make the ladies jump!' he said.

Wolfgang Amadeus Mozart, the other great master of the Classical period in music.

A scene from Mozart's opera Don Giovanni, *which combined drama and comedy in a totally new way, and revolutionized opera.*

Mozart was not nearly so lucky as Haydn in finding a sympathetic patron. After a dazzling career as a child prodigy, he was neglected, though he did enjoy some success with his operas, such as *The Marriage of Figaro* (see also page 26), *Don Giovanni* and *The Magic Flute* which have arias, or songs, that express the tenderest human emotions, of love, happiness or sorrow. When Mozart did write symphonies, concertos and string quartets, he included in the best of them more beautiful and expressive melodies, so bringing to Classical music the final touch of perfection.

Today, listening to symphonies, sonatas and string quartets in concert halls, is something we take very seriously. This is because later composers turned them into much larger, more complex and serious types of music. Also, as time went by, more people were able to go to concerts and listen attentively to music. But in the eighteenth century the situation was quite different. In the courts of Europe, they had musicians to play string quartets with breakfast and symphonies with their tea. It was all a part of gracious living.

44

A scene from another Mozart opera The Magic Flute. *Much of the opera has to do with freemasonry, which was a semi-secret society.*

6 BENEVOLENT DESPOTS

We have read how much influence philosophers and writers, artists, architects and musicians had on eighteenth-century life. This influence went right to the top, to the most powerful of rulers. It produced a small group of men and women, unique to their time and place, known as the benevolent despots. They were benevolent, by wishing to rule in a new and enlightened way, and they were despots because, like nearly all kings and queens before them, they still laid claim to the right to exercise almost total personal power. How the most famous of them tried, in different ways, to reconcile their ideals for more enlightened rule with their positions as absolute rulers, is one of the most fascinating aspects of eighteenth-century history.

Catherine the Great
Catherine the Great was a German princess married off to the heir to the Russian throne, a feeble man whom she despised. Very soon after he was crowned Tsar in 1762, she usurped the throne (and may have had a hand in his murder), and from then until her death in 1796, ruled as Catherine II, Empress of Russia.

Before her, Peter the Great had brought many changes to Russia. His biggest single achievement was the building of St Petersburg (now Leningrad), a new naval base on the Baltic Sea, which he also made Russia's capital city. Its broad streets, squares and buildings were modelled on other cities of Europe that Peter had visited and admired. Catherine also turned to other European nations for ideas and enlightenment, and especially to France. She soon had her court at St Petersburg going to see French ballet, drinking French wines and even talking in French. She herself read many works by the French *philosophes*, corresponded with Voltaire, and paid Diderot to come to St Petersburg to instruct her in art, science and philosophy. Inspired by all this learning, she convened a Legislative Commission to draw up plans for more liberal and enlightened laws.

In the end, nothing much came of Catherine's ideas for reform. A major obstacle was that she ruled over both the largest and in many ways the most backward country in Europe. Russia's population was spread thinly across thousands of miles of forest and rolling plain,

Catherine the Great of Russia, who appeared to welcome the enlightened ideas of French philosophers.

and often only by using brute force could anything be achieved. Another problem was that Catherine was involved in wars against the Turkish Ottoman Empire (winning for Russia the Crimea on the Black Sea and most of the Caucasus). She also had to deal with a serious revolt by Russia's peasants or serfs.

Catherine put her predicament well, when she said to Diderot: 'With all your great principles, which I understand very well, one would make fine books but very bad business. You forget in all your plans of reform the difference in our positions; you only work on paper, which endures all things, but I, poor Empress that I am, work on the human skin, which is irritable and ticklish to a very different degree!'

Frederick the Great of Prussia worked towards achieving a stronger and more educated Prussian state.

Frederick II, who was an able general, is seen here reviewing his troops. He is remembered more for his military successes than for his love of art and culture.

Frederick the Great

Frederick the Great of Prussia was also a lover of art and learning. He, like Catherine, was a great admirer of Voltaire and of French culture, writing essays on philosophy and a good deal of poetry all in French, which he much preferred to his own German language. He played the flute, composed symphonies and concertos, and, as we have read, brought to his court at Potsdam, near Berlin, some of the finest musicians of his time.

As a ruler he presented a very different face to the world. He hated his father (Frederick I), who had treated him most cruelly as a boy. Yet he also admired him as a model king. 'Only his care, his untiring work, his scrupulously just policies, his great and admirable thriftiness and the strict discipline he introduced made possible the achievements I have so far accomplished.'

*Frederick II (centre right) relaxing with the French philosopher,
Voltaire (seated centre left), whom he greatly admired, in the sumptuous
surroundings of Sans Souci Palace.*

Frederick the Great worked tirelessly to make Prussia—originally
a quite small and backward kingdom of gloomy pine forests by the
Baltic Sea—a strong and prosperous nation, with good government
and just laws. Freedom of religion and the beginnings of a state education system were among the reforms he introduced. But as part of
his policy, he needed to conquer the neighbouring territory of Silesia,
which would bring more industry and wealth to Prussia. This ambition
involved him in several long and bitter wars. He fought them brilliantly,
securing Silesia and a large part of Poland as well. But the legacy
of his rule was a heavy one. On his death in 1786, Frederick left Prussia
a larger and much more powerful European state. Despite his patronage of music, poetry and literature and the mostly humane laws he
introduced, it is essentially for the iron discipline of his rule and his
success as a military commander that he is remembered. 'Don't shoot
till you see the whites of the enemy's eyes', he once instructed his
troops, and it is the only phrase he is remembered by.

Louis XV

'In my person does the sovereign power rest. From me alone do my courts derive their existence and their authority. To me alone belongs legislative power.' Thus spoke King Louis XV of France. But whatever he may have claimed, in reality he rarely lived up to his own definition of a despot.

Louis had inherited the throne from his great grandfather, Louis XIV, one of the most powerful and autocratic kings who ever lived.

Louis XV, was crowned at the age of five and ruled until his death in 1774. Although he was a weak and ineffectual monarch, art and literature in France flourished during his reign.

The House of Commons in 1793, with the Prime Minister, William Pitt, addressing the House. The British parliamentary system was much admired throughout Europe.

He was not of the same calibre. As a young man, Louis XV, handsome and active, was a popular figure, known to his countrymen as Louis *le Bien-Aimé* (Louis, the Well-Loved). But he was, at heart, a pleasure-loving and rather lazy man, who soon tired of his regal duties, and left the government of France largely in the hands of others. Some of his ministers were very able men; but whenever they were seen to be attacking vested interests, by, for example, raising revenue by taxing the rich, Louis usually opted for placating the upper classes and sacked his ministers. During his long reign, from 1715 to 1774, France lost her territories in India and Canada to her great colonial rival Britain, failed to solve the financial problems of overspending, and drifted towards revolution, through failure by the crown to deal effectively with demands for constitutional reform.

The brighter side of Louis' reign was provided by some of those attached to his court, notably his mistresses, the Marquise de Pompadour and Madame du Barry, clever and cultivated women, who encouraged learning and the arts. Despite censorship, and the threat of imprisonment or exile, French writers were among the most out-spoken of the time, and made the French language the most widely used in intellectual circles everywhere. French art and design also flour-ished as never before, in the much admired style known as 'Louis Quinze' (Louis XV). The king himself was a failed despot, but France was in the forefront of enlightened countries.

Constitutional monarchy

The British monarchy in the eighteenth century was a different story altogether. Civil War and the execution of Charles I in 1649 had brought to an end the age-old notion of the 'Divine Right of Kings', according to which monarchs believed that they ruled by God-given right, and that their authority was absolute. By the beginning of the eighteenth century, the principle of a constitutional monarchy, namely that the monarch acted as head of state rather than as an absolute ruler, was established. Nearly all the British monarchs of the eighteenth century belonged to a German royal family, the Hanoverians, who were distantly related to James I of England. They reigned by general agreement rather than by any long-inherited right.

The story of British government through the century was one of gradual change in the balance of power between king and parliament. It was accompanied by the equally gradual development of party politics, in the form of two political groups called the Whigs and the Tories, and in the idea of government led by a small group of ministers (a cabinet), with one minister at their head (a prime minister). Indeed, 'gradualism' is the term used to describe the slow but more or less continuous change in British political and social life since the eighteenth century, compared with the often quite sudden and sometimes revolutionary changes experienced by many other countries.

An election scene in England in 1768. Parliamentary elections in the eighteenth-century were usually riotous and corrupt affairs, and only very few people had the right to vote in them.

Sir Robert Walpole, one of the most prominent British statesman of the eighteenth century, is generally regarded as the country's first Prime Minister.

The notable names of the time—Sir Robert Walpole, Charles James Fox, William Pitt the Elder and his son, Pitt the Younger—were all men of high social rank and wealth. Parliament itself was composed almost entirely of aristocrats and the landed gentry, and very few people had the right to vote at elections. Elections themselves were often riotous and corrupt affairs. But the manner in which power was divided between king, ministers and parliament, so that nobody became too strong or despotic, plus the freedom of speech that existed, at least among people of education and social standing, was much admired throughout Europe. 'In this country', wrote Voltaire, during his own stay in England, 'it is possible to use one's mind freely and nobly without fear and cringing.'

7 THE GRAND TOUR

Those with both wealth and leisure took part in one of the most remarkable activities of the century—the Grand Tour. For the first time in history, people travelled purely for interest or pleasure. It marked the beginning of what we now call tourism. But the Grand Tour was very different from the kind of thing most tourists expect today. The main object was not simply recreational, but rather cultural. People travelled in order to look at paintings and famous buildings, go to concerts and operas and perhaps meet famous artists, philosophers and scholars, and discuss ideas with them.

French and Italian, Dutch and German people all liked to travel, but the Grand Tour was undertaken mostly by the British. One reason for this was that there were more wealthy people in Britain in the eighteenth century than anywhere else, as a result of the rapid growth

A hazardous moment for travellers. Ship passengers were at the mercy of the elements and could be wrecked in stormy seas, often never to reach their destination.

An eighteenth-century stagecoach and inn. Stagecoaches were quite fast, but frequent stops had to be made to change or rest the horses.

of the empire, which generated an influx of trade and money into the country. In addition, most of Europe's greatest buildings and art treasures were on the Continent. Thus, if they had the time and money, British lords and ladies, merchants and bankers, their sons and daughters, might go off on a Grand Tour for a year or even longer, on what was the experience of a lifetime.

The pleasures and perils of travel
Travel in the eighteenth century was not for the faint-hearted, even under the best of circumstances. Crossing the Channel could be an ordeal in itself, travelling in small sailing ships that pitched and tossed with every wave and were at the mercy of wind and tide. 'Embarked for Calais,' wrote one traveller, 'but a strong easterly wind rising soon after we had put to sea drove us so far down the Channel that the first French port we could make was Dieppe.' If the weather deteriorated, or the tide was too strong, ships might not be able to enter the

harbour at all, and passengers had to struggle aboard or disembark from small rowing boats, with all their luggage.

The best eighteenth-century roads were paved, and the finest stage coaches might make 70 kilometres (about 40 miles) in a day, allowing for frequent stops at staging posts to change horses. But the going was rarely as good as that. The Earl of Essex described a journey he made 'in a miserable open chaise with a frame and curtains which could not keep out a little shower of rain, to which four horses were tied with cart ropes, dragging us along at the rate of three miles an hour.' Accidents were quite common. 'Crossing one of the bridges,' wrote a traveller in the French Alps, 'my friend and I had the misfortune to be overturned, and if it had not been for the railing of the bridge, the chaise might have gone complete into the river.' Less dramatically, wheels and axles were always breaking on poor, stony stretches of road, which could hold up passengers for days.

Accommodation was usually satisfactory in the big towns and cities, but out in the country it could be a different story. One young English milord who stayed at a lonely post house in Germany complained that 'our beds stank abominably and half the panes of glass in the windows were broken, so that we almost froze to death.'

Food was a problem for many travellers. Some tourists, just like their modern counterparts, objected to anything new. 'They conceal the poverty of their food with showy sauces', said one critic of French cooking. Most travellers, though, were quite happy to try new dishes

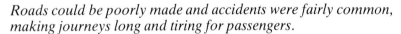

Roads could be poorly made and accidents were fairly common, making journeys long and tiring for passengers.

and were usually content. In Italy and France, they spoke of the variety and quality of fresh fruit, which in the days before refrigeration or modern packaging had to be eaten immediately.

Sickness, from bad food or drink, from colds, or more serious maladies such as dysentry and malaria, was the traveller's greatest dread. There was little that doctors could do at the best of times, and to fall sick in a foreign land was a serious plight to be in.

Places to see and things to do

Despite all the risks and hazards of eighteenth-century travel, most of those who went on a Grand Tour seem to have found it well worthwhile. There were splendid palaces, churches and art galleries to see in Spain, France, the Dutch Republic, Austria and the German kingdoms and principalities. However, the majority of tourists went to Italy. The major attractions in Florence were the Cathedral and Uffizi gallery, and in Venice, the Doges' Palace, St Mark's Cathedral and the Rialto Bridge. For those who loved the ruins of the ancient

A view of Florence, the beautiful Italian Renaissance city, from the River Arno showing the Uffizi Bridge. Florence was just one of the many cultural centres that people visited in Italy.

The Doges' Palace in the city of Venice, a destination for many people on the Grand Tour.

world, Rome was the obvious destination. The ruins of the Forum and the Colosseum made a deep impression on those who had travelled wearily for weeks or months to see them. 'I must own that these heaps of magnificent ruins', wrote one enthusiastic visitor from Rome, 'and the view of so many places renowned for the actions and fate of so many heroes, do fill the mind with great ideas of Roman grandeur and also with various reflections upon the vicissitudes of all human things.' From Rome, many seekers after antiquity went on to Naples, and nearby Herculaneum and Pompeii.

The Grand Tour also created what we should call a whole new art industry. In Venice, for example, the artist Antonio Canaletto was kept fully occupied painting his wonderfully bright and vivid views of the city to sell to rich visitors. Numerous other artists made a good living painting the portraits of ladies and gentlemen, often filling in the background with some popular romantic scene, such as the Bay of Naples (whether or not the clients had actually been there). Many tourists, in this age before the invention of photography, sketched and painted for themselves. Thousands of such souvenirs of the Grand Tour still adorn the walls of English stately homes.

It was also quite easy in those days to acquire Roman or Greek statues, sarcophagi (decorated stone coffins) and other relics of the ancient world, and have them shipped home, as unusual souvenirs. This craze for collecting Classical antiquities later reached its peak with Lord Elgin's purchase of the carved stone frieze from the temple of the Parthenon in Athens (the Elgin Marbles), now one of the world's greatest art treasures, housed in the British Museum.

The art and architecture of Italy and other continental countries made a great impression on British visitors, who saw nothing quite like it at home. Performances of music were eagerly attended for the reason that they could be compared with what British tourists heard in the opera houses or at special subscription concerts in cities such as London and Edinburgh. In Paris, one Englishman noted in his diary that he attended 'several operas, whose music pleased not my ears, though their dancing is superior.' Most British music-lovers abroad preferred Italian opera, which was closer to the style they heard at home. They were especially keen to hear, in the opera houses of Milan, Venice, Rome and Naples, the celebrated Italian castrati—men who still sang like boys. When such singers visited Britain they caused a sensation.

Opposite *The interior of Covent Garden Theatre, in London, the scene of many productions in the eighteenth century. Italian operas were particularly popular with the British.*

61

8 THE END OF THE AGE

'**W**e hold these truths to be self-evident, that all men are created equal, that they are endowed by their Creator with certain inalienable rights, that among these are Life, Liberty and the Pursuit of Happiness.' With such brave words, the American colonists made their Declaration of Independence in 1776. They were fighting to be free from British rule, and in 1781, with help from Britain's old enemy, France, they won. This victory marked the birth of the United States of America. The Constitution of the new nation was a model of its kind, based on the thinking of philosophers like Montesquieu, and on the example of British constitutional monarchy. The United States of America was the world's first modern democratic republic.

The Battle of Cowpens in 1781 took place in the final year of the American War of Independence. The American victory against the British was welcomed as a triumph for the Enlightenment.

Tom Paine and the Rights of Man

The name of the new nation was first suggested by Tom Paine, an Englishman who believed passionately in the equality and brotherhood of men, and who went to the American colonies to fight with the rebels. 'Let Americans use no other names than those of a good citizen, an

Tom Paine, the English radical Republican politician and writer, travelled to America and France to support the American War of Independence and the French Revolution.

open and resolute friend', he wrote in his book *Common Sense*. He was a close friend of Thomas Jefferson and Benjamin Franklin, principal authors of the Declaration of Independence, and of General George Washington, destined to be the nation's first president.

From America Paine went to France, to lend his support to the Revolution, which broke out in 1789. He praised the Revolution in another book, *The Rights of Man*, and called on the British people to follow the French lead, abolish their own monarchy and establish a republic.

In England, Paine was condemned as a traitor. But there were many other liberal-minded people, in Britain and elsewhere, who also welcomed these dramatic events. After all, the founding of the United States of America, and the French Revolution, with its call for 'Liberty, Equality, Brotherhood', appeared to be a fulfilment of those ideas which Voltaire, Rousseau, Kant, Bentham and most other thinkers of the Enlightenment had long upheld. It must have seemed to Paine and other idealists that with the end of the century in sight, the world really was moving towards a golden age.

The storming of the Bastille on 14 July 1789, marked the beginning of the French Revolution. The Bastille was used as a prison by the King, and was seen as a symbol of royal tyranny by the revolutionaries.

Louis XVI of France was executed on 21 January 1793, after being found guilty of treason by the republican government.

A time of upheaval

Events, though, never stand still. In France, the deposed king, Louis XVI, and Queen Marie-Antoinette, tried to escape and seek foreign help. They were captured again, put on trial and finally executed in 1793. The other monarchies of Europe, including Britain, then declared war on the young republic. The threat to France from abroad gave

The British victory at Trafalgar in 1805, a decisive sea battle of the Napoleonic Wars. It took place in a period of political instability, which marked the end of the Age of Enlightenment.

During the Industrial Revolution, people left the countryside to work in the new industrial towns.

power to such French extremists as Maximilien Robespierre, whose Committee of Public Safety instigated the Reign of Terror and the execution of thousands of innocent people. This ended with the rise of Napoleon Bonaparte who asserted the power of the military. A new European struggle developed, involving larger armies and more death and destruction than any previous wars in history. The Napoleonic Wars dragged on until 1815 when they were finally brought to an end.

Britain avoided revolution, but as the century progressed, other developments, just as significant in the long run, were at work. By the 1780s, the invention of the steam engine, the abundance of coal, the import of raw material and the easy access of manufactured goods for export, brought about the start of the Industrial Revolution. This

A French satirical drawing of a 'fashionable hairstyle' in the late eighteenth century.

generated huge new wealth, very much along the lines that Adam Smith predicted. However, the pockets of new industrial towns and cities, which were developing by the end of the eighteenth century, were to become, in the following century, the main centres of social and political unrest.

Occultism

The close of the eighteenth century was most notable for being a period of political and industrial upheaval. However, other changes were occurring. The reason, logic and healthy scepticism of the philosophers gave way to an upsurge of interest in astrology and in occult societies. An Austrian physician, Dr Anton Mesmer, offered to a gullible public his idea that powers that he called 'animal magnetism' and the 'universal fluid' were cure-alls. Count Alessandro Cagliostro claimed, like the alchemists of old, to have the elixir of life and the secret of making gold. 'Never were Rosicrucians, alchemists, prophets and everything related to them so numerous and influential', wrote one observer of Paris in 1788. 'Conversation turns almost entirely upon these matters. Looking around us we see only sorcerers, initiates, necromancers.' The writer might also have mentioned the rash of freakish costumes and hairstyles that the fashionable and rich also sported at that time.

The Romantic movement

At a deeper level, the closing years of the eighteenth century saw major changes in literary and artistic tastes. *The Castle of Otranto* by Horace Walpole (son of the British statesman Sir Robert Walpole) was a new kind of novel, full of 'gothic' imagery, which opened the way for *Frankenstein*, *Dracula* and other novels of the macabre and the bizarre. Walpole also built a large house at Strawberry Hill, by the Thames, in a style featuring turrets and battlements and exotic decoration. These changes, which came to be known as the Romantic movement, reflected a growing taste in the arts for more excitement, drama and sensationalism.

The eighteenth century had been a period of relative political stability. Throughout most of this time the Classical style in art, music and literature, which was one of order and structure, flourished. The period is also called the Age of Reason. The beginning of the Romantic movement at the end of the eighteenth century was a direct reaction against the Classical style, which the Romanticists criticized as having been rigid and formal and altogether too restrictive. The Romanticists encouraged ideas of freedom and self-expression in European art and culture. These changes, together with the political upheavals and industrial developments, all served to emphasize a break with the past, and with it, the end of the Age of Enlightenment.

Horace Walpole's large house at Strawberry Hill by the Thames, built in a Neo-Gothic style, reflected the growing interest in Romanticism at the end of the eighteenth century.

DATE CHART

1702	Start of War of Spanish Succession, Britain and Austria against France.
1704	British victory at Battle of Blenheim.
1709	Dr Samuel Johnson born.
1713	End of War of Spanish Succession. Denis Diderot born.
1714	Coronation of George I of Britain.
1715	Louis XIV of France dies. Succeeded by Louis XV. First Jacobite Rebellion.
1724	Immanuel Kant born.
1727	George I dies. Succeeded by George II.
1731	Daniel Defoe dies.
1732	Joseph Haydn born.
1740	Coronation of Frederick the Great of Prussia, and of the Empress Maria Theresa of Austria.
1745	Second Jacobite Rebellion, defeated at Battle of Culloden Moor (1746). Jonathan Swift dies.
1750	J. S. Bach dies.
1756	Start of Seven Years' War, Britain and Prussia against France, Austria and Russia. W. A. Mozart born.
1759	British victory at Quebec. G. F. Handel dies.
1760	George II dies. Succeeded by George III.
1762	Coronation of Catherine the Great of Russia.
1763	End of Seven Years' War.
1764	William Hogarth dies.
1774	Louis XV dies. Succeeded by Louis XVI.
1775	Start of American War of Independence.
1776	American Declaration of Independence.
1778	Voltaire dies.
1780	Empress Maria Theresa dies.
1781	British surrender at Yorktown and end of American War of Independence.
1784	Denis Diderot and Samuel Johnson die.
1786	Frederick the Great dies.
1789	Storming of the Bastille and start of French Revolution.
1791	Mozart dies.
1796	Catherine the Great dies.

GLOSSARY

Baroque Style of architecture, art and music, from about 1600 to 1730, very grand and rich. The word originally meant a pearl of large or irregular shape.

Chinoiserie Style of decoration or fine art based on imitations of Chinese designs.

Classical Style of architecture, art and music, from about 1700 to 1800, in which pure beauty, in form and style, mattered most. Named after Classical or ancient Greece and Rome.

Concerto Musical composition, usually for a solo instrument and orchestra. The Italian word for 'playing together'.

Constitutional monarch King or queen acting as head of state rather than the ruler of a country.

Despot Ruler with complete personal power, a kind of dictator. From the Greek *despotes*, 'master' or 'lord'.

Empiricism Philosophy arguing that experience is the only way of gaining knowledge and understanding. Put at its simplest, 'seeing is believing'.

Fresco Type of painting done on fresh, damp plaster. Italian word for 'cool, fresh'.

Frieze Band of decoration, usually between the top of a wall and ceiling or roof.

Jacobite Rebellions Two uprisings, of 1715 and 1745, by supporters of the Scottish Catholic heirs to the British throne. Jacobite means 'of King James'.

Laissez-faire French expression meaning 'allow to do', applied mainly to a policy of free trade and business with no controls or regulations.

Occultism Belief in and the study and practice of magic, mysticism, the supernatural and astrology.

Oratorio Musical composition for orchestra, chorus and soloists usually based on a religious theme.

Pediment In Classical architecture, broad triangular-shaped part of a building, usually above columns, doors or windows.

Pillory Instrument of punishment, in which head and hands were clamped between boards.

Rationalism Philosophical doctrine prevalent in the eighteenth century that knowledge is acquired by reason alone rather than through experience.

Rococo Style of architecture, art and music, from about 1700 to 1750, highly decorative, graceful and delicate. The word means 'rocky', in the sense of many shapes and sizes.

Romantic Style or movement in the arts and literature following the Classical period, with personal feeling more important than beauty and form.

Rosicrucians Members of an esoteric religious order, which venerates the emblem of the rose and Cross as symbols of Christ's Resurrection and Redemption and which is devoted to occult lore.

Satire Use of ridicule and irony in novels and plays to expose and scorn issues and individuals.

Sonata Musical composition, for solo piano or one or two instruments, with several individual pieces or 'movements'. Sonata form is a special way of writing a single piece of music. From the Italian *suonare*, 'to sound'.

Stocks Instrument of punishment, in which the feet were clamped between boards.

Symphony Musical composition for orchestra, usually of four individual pieces, or 'movements'. From the Greek words meaning 'harmonious sounding'.

Utilitarianism Philosophy of usefulness and practicability in politics and economics.

FURTHER READING

Anderson, M. S. *Europe in the Eighteenth Century, 1713–1783* Longman, 1976

Black, Jeremy *The British and the Grand Tour* Croom Helm Press, 1985

Hart, Roger *English Life in the Eighteenth Century* Wayland, 1970

Rudé, George *Europe in the Eighteenth Century: Aristocracy and the Bourgeois Challenge* Weidenfeld & Nicolson, 1972

White, R. J. *Europe in the Eighteenth Century* Macmillan, 1965

There are also many fine biographies of the famous men and women of the age, and books on eighteenth-century art and architecture.

PICTURE ACKNOWLEDGEMENTS

The illustrations were supplied by: The Bridgeman Art Library *cover*; John Freeman & Co 24, 25, 34, 35; The Mansell Collection 13, 15, 20, 21, 30, 32, 42, 43, 47, 54, 55, 65; Mary Evans Picture Library 6, 7, 9, 14, 16, 19, 22, 23, 28, 29, 31, 33, 38, 40, 41, 44, 45, 48, 49, 50, 51, 52, 53, 56, 57, 58, 59, 62, 63, 66, 70; Wayland Picture Library 4, 5, 8, 10, 11, 17, 27, 36, 39, 61, 64, 67, 68.

INDEX